Praise for *The Law of Radiance*

I loved this book. It's like the missing piece in the jigsaw of the universal truths. It's an easy-to-read, easy-to-use guide to a more fulfilling and abundant life. The author draws on her many years of experience as a clairvoyant and weaves in the wisdom taken from her personal journey to create a book that will help anyone to become their more radiant self.

—Joanna Crosse, presentation and voice coach, and author of *Find Your Voice*

The Law of Radiance is a very beautiful and special book. Each time I read it, I learn more and am reminded of the power and Source within each one of us. We are more than we think we are, and *The Law of Radiance* greatly helps to connect us with our Higher Self and Divinity. This is inspired writing, and I am so glad I have read it and felt the connection with my own radiance as well as recognising it in others as a result. Thank you!

—Ysanne Lewis, internationally recognised astrologer and author of *The Time Catcher*

THE LAW OF
RADIANCE

THE LAW OF
RADIANCE

Before and Essential to
The Law of Attraction

Anne M. Hassett

Pecoraro Sullivan
Publishing Company

Dedicated, with immense gratitude,
to the Enlightened Ones
who have come throughout history
to show us the way home.

Library of Congress Cataloging-in-Publication Data
Hassett, Anne M.
The Law of Radiance
1. New Age 2. Spirituality
ISBN: 978-988-78868-6-0 (paperback)
ISBN: 978-988-78868-7-7 (ePub)
ISBN: 978-988-78868-8-4 (Kindle)

Pecoraro Sullivan Publishing Company
P. O. Box 7892, General Post Office, Hong Kong
www.PSpub.Co

Contents

The Temple of the Sacred Heart

To All Who Enter Here, Welcome Home!

As you enter the temple of your sacred heart, rejoice. You have been drawn to this book by your Divine Self. Your yearning for something better, something more, is being answered. You have called out, "Is this it? Is this all there is?", and you have wondered what it is all about and why there is so much suffering and struggle.

Your Soul has drawn you to this book so that you may be reminded of what you have forgotten. You have forgotten that you are part of Source, a spark of the Divine, the child of the Great Creator. You will learn to *radiate* positive creative energy to *attract* to you all that is good and healthy and joyful. You will remember why you do not have to struggle.

You have wandered away from the bliss that was originally yours, and you have traversed the realms of darkness, struggle and limitation. Your anguished cries have reached out into the cosmos.

You have been heard. In the pages of this book, you will be lovingly reminded of your original greatness and unlimitedness. As you read, read slowly. Go into the temple that is within your beautiful sacred heart, and meet your radiant Higher Self within. This is the real you, the you that has been waiting for the separated and lost part of yourself to return. Your sacred heart is part of Source's sacred heart. Source can be individualised but not divided.

There is but One.

And, as you find yourself again and begin to *radiate* your light, recognise the Divine in those around you and remind them, too. Be the shining beacon for them.

Show them the way home!

Foreword

Why *The Law of Radiance*? I was meditating some months ago, and the Law of Attraction came to mind. A little voice in my head whispered, "To really *attract*, you must *radiate* that which you wish to *attract*". *Radiation* and *attraction* are a powerful dynamic. One cannot work without the other.

As I pondered on this, I realised that, yes, one cannot attract *having* something from a place of *not having* that something, because the immutable Law of Attraction *will attract* that which is like itself. *Like attracts like*, and that *attraction* works in every aspect of our lives, whether it be health, loving relationships, abundant prosperity or anything else.

It is difficult to *radiate* good health when we are ill or *prosperity* when we are down to our last penny. But it can be done through a shift of consciousness, and that is what this book is all about.

In a nutshell, we must radiate *that which we wish to* attract.

At first, I wanted to call this book *The Law of RADIATION*, as that is what it really is, but my friends pointed out that this could be a very off-putting title; it smacks of nuclear fallout, atom bombs and toxic emissions. So, it has become *The Law of Radiance*. But bear in mind that *radiation* is much nearer the truth of what I am attempting to convey. The repetition of ideas and concepts in this book is deliberate to emphasise the point. I hope that you will not just read this book straight through. I hope that you will stop and think from point to point, embody the concepts and ideas, and put them into use so that you can become all that you were meant to be. Or should I say *return* to your true glory and 're-*member*' the powerful being you truly are but have forgotten. Embrace your true Higher Nature, and watch your life *change*.

I am not a religious person—I prefer to call myself a *spiritual* person. I do not subscribe to any organised religious belief system, even though I respect the fundamental truths in all of them and have learned so much from the study of many religious beliefs and doctrines. I was brought up Catholic and have a deep and abiding love for the one who was called Master Jesus. His teachings are as valid today as they were two thousand years ago; perennial truth stands outside of time and space.

It is interesting that nowhere in the teachings of this august teacher and miracle worker does he say that he is Source—only that he said, "Know ye not that *ye* are gods and sons of the Most High", meaning that we are all gods. He did all in his power to teach us that.

In my life today, I try to embrace the Source Self that we all have and are, and I try not to operate from the limited perspective of ego; we are all both Source Self and ego. When I am operating from the Source portion and not from the ego, my life is so much better. The purpose of this book is to share those ideas with you so that you, too, can have a far, far better life.

I believe in Source, whatever you conceive that power to be. Call it Universe, Allah, Higher Power, Source, Divine Spirit, All-That-Is. The Native Americans called it 'Great Mystery', which just about sums it up. In this book, I mostly use the name Source so as not to offend anybody's beliefs. Source has no need of names. He/She/It is beyond names. It is we, us humans, who have need of names as we communicate through language.

Through my search for meaning in life, I have read and studied the works of many masters. They all carry the same message, albeit a message geared towards cultural and geographic conditions, and different eras.

Whoever Jesus was, he was a great teacher, and his teachings—read in the light of what we know today regarding quantum physics and creating our own reality—contain all the instructions to create Heaven on Earth. He said, "I am come that ye may have life and have it more abundantly".

All of the great teachers—Lao Tzu, Buddha, Jesus, Sivananda and many others—taught more or less the same basic idea: that our true nature is Divine and that we create our own reality by our thoughts, beliefs and the energy we *radiate* out from our own being, which in turn *attracts* the circumstances of our lives. Basically, we are both Divine and human; human controlled by ego. The ego is that little limited concept of self. It is the false self. The true self is the Higher Self: our Soul or Spirit.

So much of what the great masters taught has fallen on deaf ears or been distorted by human egos in search of power and glory. With the discovery of quantum physics, we now have the modern scientific validation for these long-taught wisdoms. Certainly, much of what we see is not real.

We know that appearances are deceptive. We know that the Earth is not flat, the Earth is not the centre of the universe, and matter is not solid. We are learning and growing in every way, and we are waking up... we are waking as if from a long sleep, and we are questioning old paradigms.

The truth of our being is Divine. We are Source incarnate. Spirit is the life force within us. It is our *BE-ing-ness*. The living, breathing essence that is our *BE*-ing is our life. If we did not have that within us, we would be physically dead. At the time of physical death, that life force leaves the physical body and our Soul or Spirit continues in another form.

We are pure Spirit, temporarily inhabiting human bodies; Earth suits, while we are here! The Divine Essence that dwells within and through our physical body is Source. Source not only dwells within us, but we also live and move and have our *BE*-ing within it. Source is *us* in the absolute.

The true essence of who we are is infinite; the truth of who we are is unlimited. Therefore, our essence is unlimited love. It is unlimited prosperity. It is unlimited health and wellbeing. It is unlimited vitality. That is what we are. That is the truth of our *BE*-ing. "And the truth shall set you free!"

Why, then, do we experience a lack and limitation of every kind? Why are we poor or sick or feeling unloved? Those limiting feelings come from the finite aspect of ourselves: our ego. The ego was originally created to take care of our basic survival needs, but, some-how, it has got out of hand. The majority of humanity knows nothing of its true nature; nothing of our inherent Divinity lives solely from the ego.

The world is controlled by egos, and what a fine mess it has got us into! Egos—because the ego believes in limitation—feel that there is not enough to go around. Therefore, egos have to compete... have to fight for what egos believe are limited resources (because we fight for what we perceive are limited resources). We have war and competition everywhere. We are killing our planet through the results of our greed, and all because we believe that there is not enough to go around. Our egos' senses deceive us.

The universe is unlimited. Source is unlim-ited. And so, because we are Source in embodiment, we create what we believe— those beliefs *radiate* out from us to *attract* the circumstances and conditions of our lives. We can create anything we believe in. As most of us, operating from ego and not from the Source Self, believe in limitation, we create it. It *can* be different.

It is our beliefs *radiating* out from us that attract the desired outcome, provided we *radiate* what we desire and not what we do not desire. We must *radiate* to *attract*, and it behoves us to monitor very carefully what we are *radiating*. In other words, we must watch our thoughts. Many great teachers have incarnated over the millennia to remind us of our Source-ness and to teach us about who we are and what we are capable of. They even demonstrated the results of what they were teaching: they performed miracles. We didn't quite get it. Instead, some tried to make these teachers into gods and founded whole belief systems around them.

Thankfully, because of the shifting paradigm of the age we are entering, so many are waking up. So many Souls are remembering their origin and their true nature. Massive change is afoot. Because we are all connected—we are all part of Source and, therefore, cannot be separate from Source— as one of us wakes, it has a knock-on effect in waking up the rest of humanity.

Nothing is predictable or inevitable. The future is not written in stone. We are creating our future all the time by our thoughts, beliefs and actions. Psychics, like myself, can see the forthcoming events in a person's life, and if there is no change in the person's consciousness or outlook, they will travel along to that particular destination. But as we step into Higher Consciousness, take responsibility and become aware of the truth of who we are, instead of letting the limited ego run the show, we realise who we are and we step into mastery. We can then create a *new* and *better* destination. We recognise that we are creators, not victims. The same goes for astrology: astrology is the map or the prevailing weather conditions that we have to navigate and the innate strengths and weaknesses that each of us possess on a human level, but the power is still in our hands—or in our consciousness of who we are. When we operate from Higher Consciousness, all limitations fall away.

"The fault, dear Brutus, is not in our stars,
But in ourselves, that we are underlings".
—William Shakespeare

Because we are all part of the whole, as each of us changes, we change the whole. We then *radiate* a new frequency into the grid of the field of infinite possibility that surrounds us all. So, there is no need to go out and change the world, or indeed save the world; as Buddha said, "Let there be change, and let it begin with me".

Many on the planet today are achieving mastery. Now, we too can aspire to it. It is but a thought away. We have, at this time on the planet, with all the knowledge at our disposal, a unique opportunity to move forward in Divine wisdom to create Heaven here on Earth. Let us lift our consciousness to one of love, health, prosperity, peace and harmony, and then let's *radiate*!

Namaste
(Namaste means *I bow to the Divine in you.*)

The Law of Radiance

"As above, so below. As within, so without".
   —The Emerald Tablet (Circa 3,000 BC)

In the world of personal growth and self-help, there are few who have not heard of the Law of Attraction. It is part of most books, courses and workshops involving manifestation or creating your own reality.

The Law of Attraction works—there is no doubt about it. Why, then, do so many well-meaning and earnest students of life cry out that, despite spending hours daily making positive affirmations, creating vision boards, putting Post-it notes on the fridge or the vanity mirror and making manifestation lists, what they are trying to *attract* into their lives is just not happening?

The Law of Attraction is working all the time. If we want it to manifest our desires, we have to change—not our thinking, but our very own consciousness. We usually approach the manifestation process from a place of *not having* whatever it is we are trying to attract into our lives.

We are separated from that which we wish to *attract*. We are *here*, and what we want to *attract* is out *there*. We feel that the Law of Attraction will magnetise our desire to us, but the Law of Attraction works entirely on the principle of *like attracts like*, so of course the law works. It *attracts* back to us that which we are missing. The Law of Attraction reflects our state of mind. It mirrors our state of consciousness. In the matter of vibes, the universe will always 'return to sender'!

Like attracts like. It is the nature of all things to be drawn to similar frequencies. For example, we want to *attract* love because we feel unloved. From that place of feeling unloved, we make affirmations or we work on changing our beliefs, but we are still *radiating* that unloved state of being, so we can only *attract*

26

more of the same. We must change from a state of lack of love to one of feeling loving and being loved. We must *radiate* the love frequency. Loving and being loved is our birth right and our natural state.

Or we want to *attract* more money into our lives because we are in a state of 'not having enough'. The whole reason we are trying to *attract* more money is because not only do we believe that we do not have 'enough' but we *feel* it, we *live* it, we *act* it and we *think* it. In fact, we *are* it. We act it out in all that we do. We toss and turn in bed at night worrying about paying the next big bill, or we scrimp and save for a rainy day. We deny ourselves pleasures and luxuries because we have an inner poverty consciousness. To move from a poverty consciousness to one of abundance, we must *radiate* abundance. Abundant prosperity is our birth right and our natural state.

A poverty consciousness will never *attract* wealth—only more poverty. We have to *be* that wealth, not just *think* it, not just *believe* it, not even just *feel* it, but actually *BE* it. How do we do that? We think abundance and *know* that it is our true nature: we do not entertain any thoughts of *lack*, and we surrender our lives to our Higher Self/Source, then we *radiate* that which we wish to receive by *believing* that it is already ours, thus developing a consciousness of *having* so that the Law of Attraction begins to work in our favour and not against us.

The same principle applies to our health and wellbeing. We fret and worry about developing cancer or Alzheimer's because "everybody is getting it"—or so the media and the collective consciousness would have us believe! When winter comes, we expect to get colds and flu. We *radiate* or *project* that thought out into the field, and the Law of Attraction reflects back to us our state of consciousness, and—surprise, surprise—we get flu. To overcome this, we need to *act*, *feel*, *think* and *be* perfect health. We must develop a consciousness of health and wholeness. We must *radiate* wellbeing. Perfect health is our birth right and our natural state.

The universe always says "Yes".

The Universe Always Says "Yes"

For the Law of Attraction to work for us in our lives, we must *radiate* that which we wish to *attract*. *Like attracts like*, so the Law of Radiance must come *before* the Law of Attraction.

Loving and being loved, being in a fulfilling career, having perfect health and having abundant wealth are our natural states, but we have deviated from our natural state of being. It is *natural* for us to be *radiantly* healthy, rich, fulfilled and to enjoy life to the full.

To be otherwise is *unnatural*. It is good for us to develop enthusiasm for life and for living. The word 'enthusiasm' comes from the Greek word *entheos*, meaning to be filled with 'Source'.

We get off track because we have forgotten our Divine nature. Blaming or condemning ourselves for this is unhelpful and unnecessary; we just need to reconnect to the *truth* of our being and allow all false conditions to fall away.

We have lost our connection. We have forgotten who we are. Perhaps, deep down, the enormity of our power scares us. We have been taught for so long that we are puny and powerless while all the while our greatness hides within just waiting to be recognised. (Re-*cognised*.)

Marianne Williamson, in her wonderful book *A Return to Love* sums it up nicely:

"Our deepest fear is not that we are inadequate. Our deepest fear is that we are powerful beyond measure. We were born to make manifest the glory of God that is within us".

The biblical story of the prodigal son is allegorical. It is the story of us wandering away from our Father/Mother/Source, thinking we can do better alone. We are then operating from the small—the ego. The ego has little to no real *power*, so we get ourselves into lack, loss and limitation. In desperation, we try to find our way back to 'the Father's house'. When we have suffered enough, we will try anything and everything. 'The Father's house' is our state of returning to our true essence, to recognising and re-embodying the consciousness of our all-powerful, omniscient, omnipotent Self. The big 'I'.

In the parable, as the 'son' approached the Father's house, the Father came out to meet him. The meaning here is that when we develop a desire to raise our consciousness to one of embodiment of our Higher Self, we go back to 'the Father's house' and the 'Father' (our Higher Self) comes to meet us and leads us back to 'the Father's house'. Then, 'the 'Father', our real Higher Self, showers us with riches and abundant gifts. In the story, there is a feast prepared to welcome back the errant 'son'.

Jesus, who is like our big brother, was an enlightened being—a 'Christed' one. He came to *teach* us *truth*, to wake us up to our true *identity*. At the time in which he lived, using the word 'Father' was understood by the people of that time. 'Father' is Source; the Source from whence we came and who we are created in the image and likeness of.

When Jesus healed, turned water into wine, and performed the miracle of the loaves and fishes, he was operating from his 'Father' within. He Himself said, "Of myself I can do nothing, it is the Father in me that doeth the works". In other words, he was teaching us that from our little ego-/personality-selves, we can do little, but when we connect from and embody the consciousness of the *truth* of our *being*, which is our Higher Self—part of Source—then we can create our own miracles.

Know Thyself

"Your sole business in life is to attain God-realisation. All else is useless and worthless".
—*Sivananda*

W ritten at the entrance to The Oracle of Delphi's temple, the admonition 'know thyself' has been given to us thousands of years ago. Why? Because we have become lost. Lost in the illusion of limitedness. It is an illusion. The eastern mystical teachers called it 'maya'. According to the ancient Hindu Vedic texts:

"Maya is the veil that covers our real nature and the real nature of the world around us. Maya is fundamentally inscrutable: we don't know why it exists and we don't know when it began. What we do know is that, like any form of ignorance,

maya ceases to exist at the dawn of knowledge, the knowledge of our own Divine nature.

"Brahman is the real truth of our existence: in Brahman we live, move, and have our being. 'All this is indeed Brahman', the Upanishads—the scriptures that form Vedanta philosophy—declare.

"The changing world that we see around us can be compared to the moving images on a movie screen: without the unchanging screen in the background, there can be no movie. Similarly, it is the unchanging Brahman—the substratum of existence—in the background of this changing world that gives the world its reality.

"Yet for us this reality is conditioned, like a warped mirror, by time, space, and causality—the Law of Cause and Effect. Our vision of reality is further obscured by wrong identification: we identify ourselves with the body, mind, and ego rather than the Atman, the Divine Self.

"This original misperception creates more ignorance and pain in a domino effect: identifying ourselves with the body and mind, we fear disease, old age, and death; identifying ourselves with the ego, we suffer from anger, hatred, and a

hundred other miseries. Yet none of this affects our real nature: the Atman."

A possible creation idea...

Before time began, there was Source—just Source and nothing else. Source of Itself could not know Itself, so It decided to expand, to send out bits of Itself, so we had Genesis/the big bang/the out-breathing of Brahma/Creation. Source sent out zillions and zillions of bits of Itself into the void. Some of those bits became galaxies, planets, etc. Physicality was *created.* Some of those bits became *us!* Originally, we remembered who and what we were: fragments of Source, made in the image and likeness of our Creator, because after all, we were bits of our Creator.

For eons, we floated about enjoying ourselves, remembering who and what we were. We created things; we had fun. We played with matter and physicality. Then, we looked at physicality and decided to explore it, and so in we came. We immersed ourselves in the physical, but we still remembered who we were. We were still having fun. We created our egos to take charge of the nitty-gritty of our lives while we—our Higher Selves—could observe the experiment of becoming physical beings. We appointed the ego as our PA, our personal assistant.

The ego, originally intended to be our servant, developed an inflated notion of its own importance and decided it wanted to become the master. Then, as time went on and as we became more and more enamoured of the physical, the ego took more and more control, and we forgot our true identity. There are even some today who think that the physical is all there is! Know anyone like that?

The physical is made up of positive and negative, in the electrical sense: it is a state of duality. Therefore, we have dark and light, up and down, here and there. We ate of the tree of 'good and evil'. This is how our egos began to believe in sickness and death and limitation of all kinds. We banished ourselves from the garden of Eden: our true state.

Forgetting who we were and disconnecting ourselves from Source was the original sin. Time and time again, great teachers like Buddha, Jesus, Lao Tzu, Krishna and others who had not forgotten who we were came to remind us, to wake us up from our sleep of immersion in the physical. For a time, we got part of their message; we took steps upwards in our evolution. Then, our egos, our little human selves, distorted the message, and all kinds of structures and dogmas and institutions grew up around what was intended as a simple message of *truth*. The message of *truth* is that we are Divine beings, unlimited in all things.

In Hermetic tradition, it is said that everything is a manifestation of Spirit. This also ties up with the holographic theory; the whole is contained in every part, therefore in every part is the power and the possibility of the whole. We are all a part of Source, and our Higher Selves as fragments of Source are connected to Source and have access to all that Source is. That means that our Higher Selves are unlimited and eternal: *made in the image and likeness of Source.*

Aha! As we realise the truth of our being, all falsehood falls away, all limitation dissolves. If we could truly get the message of who and what we really are, our lives would become perfect. If, as it is said, we are sparks of the

Divine or fragments (bits) of Source, made in the image and likeness of our Creator, how could we ever be sick, poor, sad or lonely? It would not be possible. If I am Source being me and you are Source being you, then the *truth* of who we really are is perfection.

The *reality* of Source is perfection. Source cannot be sick, poor or limited in any way: it is impossible. There is no *need* to strive. No *need* for all that effort. The Higher Self takes very good care of us. So, the trick is to remember who we are and to operate *only* from that reality. We have been so programmed for millennia that we find it difficult to make that shift of perception; the ego has held sway for too long. But we can 'get it' in the twinkling of an eye when we call the ego's bluff.

"Be careful what you water your dreams with. Water them with worry and fear and you will produce weeds that choke the life from your dream. Water them with optimism and solutions and you will cultivate success. Always be on the lookout for ways to turn a problem into an opportunity for success. Always be on the lookout for ways to nurture your dream".

—*Lao Tzu*

When we operate from our Higher Self (Source Self), we are perfect and all around us will reflect that. It is the ego that wants us to keep 'working on ourselves'. The very concept of 'working on ourselves' implies that we are *imperfect*—flawed, not good enough. That is the ego's strategy: to keep itself in control.

As we surrender to the Higher Self, the perfection manifests in all areas. So, to reach that perfection, the way is to totally surrender. We need to stop striving and instead allow the Higher Self to be in charge of our lives. Don't go to battle with the ego and Higher Self. Just make a decision as to *who* is going to be in *control*. Make a decision that the Higher Self takes up its rightful place as the boss. Connect with and be aware of Higher Self, and hand over everything. Everything. No exceptions.

Many courses and workshops today, run by well-meaning people, put the emphasis on attaining our goals. Goals are for the ego. Goals to *have* more, to be *better* than others, to have 'trappings'. This attitude can only stem from the ego's belief in not *having* enough or not *being* enough. Our Master Self/Higher Self knows no lacking and can only experience wealth, success and happiness. Until we wake up to the *truth* of our *being*, we still act from the personality level, and goals are okay at this level. As we become aware of our Source Self and we remember who we are, the whole game changes.

We just need to wake up. We need to replace goals with *visions* and remember that what we desire is already in existence; all we have to do is allow the barriers of doubt, fear and belief in our own limitedness to fall away. The important thing is to allow the barriers we have erected through our fear and our ignorance of the ultimate truth. The ultimate truth is that we *are* Source expressing Itself *as* us. We just need to vision our perfection and allow Source to express *as* that in us.

"Where there is no vision, the people perish:
but he that keepeth the law, happy is he".
—*Proverbs 29:18*

Our main purpose is to raise our consciousness. Master Jesus said, "Seek ye first the kingdom of Heaven, and all these things shall be added unto you". Then He added, "The Kingdom of Heaven is within".

Our level of consciousness determines our state of Heaven or Hell, and it is here on Earth, not in some other reality. We take our state of consciousness with us wherever we go.

Surrender

*"Always say 'yes' to the present moment.
What could be more futile, more insane, than to
create inner resistance to what already is? What
could be more insane than to oppose life itself,
which is now and always now? Surrender to
what is. Say 'yes' to life—and see how life
suddenly starts working for you rather than
against you."*

—*Eckhart Tolle*

We need to surrender: surrender to Source. It is interesting how we resist handing over our will and our lives to our Higher Source. Do we really believe that we, from our limited little ego self, can deliver a better way of life than Source can? The idea is insane. Source only wants the very best for us. There can never be a power that is separate from us that is greater than the Source power within us. That power is within and without and everywhere, from the deepest part of our inner Self to the farthest reaches of the universe. We are never separate from it—only in our minds. We can become more consciously aware of this power at any time and *radiate* that power out from us to magnetise our good to us. Our egos' resistance to our good and our belief in our unworthiness is what causes us pain, disease, scarcity and other limitations. When we totally surrender, our lives become immeasurably better. We surrender by going into our sacred heart.

We can invite our Divine Higher Self to dissolve the negative beliefs and remove our shortcomings. As we progress ever higher on our journey to reconnecting with our Divine Self, as we become more aware of our faults, and as our failings become more obvious, we can become discouraged, and we may slip back into feelings of unworthiness. Some refer to this as 'the ego's last stand'. The ego begins to feel it is losing its grip, and so it will do all in its power to stop us progressing.

It will remind us of our perceived unworthiness. It will tell us things like, "Life is hard", and, "You have to survive". Survival is fear based and does not acknowledge the infinite Source of all good that we are a part of and which is part of our inherent *nature*. Suffering and pain come from not surrendering to a power greater than our limited, fearful ego selves.

We need to remember that Source is the *source* and *substance* of all our good—not work, not other people, not any human power. Those are but the channels through which Source pours its beneficence into our lives. Source knows our needs and will always find a way to give us what we need, to let us do the things we enjoy—and the money or provision comes, anyway. We are always beautifully taken care of. As we know this and *radiate* this knowing, the universe responds in magical ways. The important thing is that our *knowing* or *belief* must be greater than our fear or doubts.

What can we do to make our own lives a 'Heaven on Earth'? We can take time out during the day. Just a few minutes is all it takes. There is no need to sit in the lotus position for hours or to perform elaborate rituals. When we can truly remember who we are and keep that awareness of our Source-ness in our daily lives, we need not strive to develop our psychic powers or learn a new and better healing technique; our True Self, the Spirit within, is already super psychic and has all the healing powers one could ever need. Jesus, who prophesied and healed and performed miracles, said, "These things that I do, ye shall do them but in greater measure". He did not lie. One of the greatest acts of healing we can perform is to remind each other of who we truly are, keep waking one another up and not allow ourselves to go back to the limited consciousness of ego.

To move away from ego limitation and into mastery, all we need to do is to take a minute or two, close our eyes and become aware of the Spirit within (Source). See that Spirit within as a light in the heart area, and *know* that that is who we truly are. *Allow* that Divine Light to dissolve all limitations. Let it dissolve the limitations on the physical level of our lives: the financial lack and the physical ailments. Let it also dissolve the limitations of our thoughts and our limiting belief systems. Let us surrender our ego's will.

This awareness is to be without struggle. Does a rose struggle to bloom? Does a cloud struggle to float in the sky? Do the ocean waves struggle to lap against the shore? No. They just *are.* Some of the great teachers and philosophers who seemed to abound in the thirties—folk like Ernest Holmes, Emmet Fox, Joel S. Goldsmith and many others—continually exhorted their followers to 'practice the Presence'. Then, we *radiate* that peace and joy of our Source-ness out to *attract* more peace and joy into our lives and the lives of those around us.

Three to five minutes, several times a day, can and *will* make a huge difference in our lives. No longer is it necessary to 'work on ourselves' or strive or struggle in any way. Once we realise (*real*-ise = make real) the truth of who we are, all need for struggle falls away. Surrender is not giving up; it is an act of allowing the greater power—Source—to manage our affairs.

Simple? Yes. Easy? Maybe not. It will be whatever we believe it to be. We have become, over aeons, so entrenched in limiting belief systems and indoctrinated with limiting ideas about who we are, that it takes a little time to change. Let's make it easy. Let's make it gentle and flowing. Let's approach it like a feather dancing on the breeze. Easy it may be, but as we have become accustomed to the ego's programme of restriction and limited thinking, it is important to be aware and focussed. Constantly bringing our attention gently back to our Source-ness will, over time, become a new habit to replace the ego's tyrannical rule.

No effort is required. It is a gentle process of saying to oneself, while *feeling* it and *knowing* it, "The truth of my being is unlimited *love*. The truth of my being is unlimited *vitality*. The truth of my being is unlimited *abundance*. It is what I am. As I am Source being me, there can be no lack or limitation of any kind". It is important not to let the saying of this be an empty repetition of affirmations. It is best if it is an *awareness.* Soon, we will not even need the words. The *knowingness* within will take care of it all.

Meditation to Surrender

Find a quiet space, and make sure you will not be disturbed. Relax all the muscles of your body. *Visualise* yourself in the temple of your sacred heart where your Divine Self/Source resides. In that glorious, light-filled space, take a deep, deep breath, then formulate the intention of deepening your conscious contact and awareness of your very own Divine Self—that part of Source that you are. Feel the warm, unconditional loving embrace of your *true* essence—the part of you that is Divine and all powerful.

In that quiet space of pure love, just listen. Let go of all distracting thoughts of the ego mind, and listen to the soft and gentle voice of Source. Do not force, do not rush, do not try. Just *be*. As the noisy chatter of the ego mind abates, listen. Listen to the voice of the inner silence in which your Soul speaks to you. Taking another deep breath, feel your entire being fill with love and gratitude, and say "thank you, thank you, thank you". Say "thank you" for just *being* and say "thank you" for anything that comes to mind.

Then, with another deep breath, surrender everything to Source. Everything. Holding nothing back, let go, and let Source flow.

In the consciousness of this expression of love and gratitude, our vibration and frequency are raised to new heights. We then *radiate* this high frequency vibration, and, in so doing, we set the Law of Attraction in motion to *attract* to us ever greater good. Practicing this meditation, even if only for a few minutes every day, can radically change our lives. Imagine what doing it several times a day can do for us!

This meditation is to be done not with the intention of *making* something happen but rather of raising our consciousness to a vibration where good things are bound to happen because we are *radiating* from a place of joy and gratitude, and from our Divine Higher Self. The mirror of life will always reflect our state of consciousness. Then, the Law of Radiance and The Law of Attraction work in perfect harmony to out-picture the good we seek.

Surrender

"Be content with what you have;
rejoice in the way things are.
When you realise there is nothing lacking,
the whole world belongs to you".

—*Lao Tzu*

I Λm

"Ignorance of our true nature creates suffering".
—The Gospel of Mary Magdalene

There is the big I and the little i. The big I is that part of us that lives outside of time and space. It is an aspect or fragment of Source. Some call it Higher Self, Higher Power, Christ Consciousness, Master Self or Holy Spirit within. It is the individualisation of Source. 'Individual' means something that cannot be further divided. It is the I AM awareness. It is the sacred Ohm. It is omniscient and omnipotent. Love is its essence and state. Source can be individualised but never divided.

When we pray or meditate, this is the consciousness of Self that we need to be aware of. This is where our true and only power lies. True prayer is meditating on the Higher Self. Some call it 'practising the Presence'. Kneeling and pleading to Source that we think is separate from us is keeping us distanced from Source. Source is *All*, and we are part of that *All*, not distinct nor separate. We are like drops of water in the ocean, each drop having its own unique individuality but part of the ocean, nonetheless. It is the ego's arrogance to think otherwise.

The little *i* is the *false creation*. The Satan of the senses. It is the deceiver. We will refer to it as 'ego'. (Ego is said by some to be the state when we *E*ase *G*od *O*ut!) It deceives us into the limiting beliefs that miscreate the perceived lack in our lives. It is paranoid and delusional. It gives its power away to outside influences. Like a child, when things go wrong, the ego seldom takes responsibility. It blames everyone and everything, and, in its fear and paranoia, it hugs its limitedness and victimhood ever closer.

To survive, the ego has to maintain its separateness. That is its identity. Therefore, to keep that identity, it has to create a sense of 'otherness'. What is not 'me' as an ego has to be 'other'. The ego does this by judging and criticising. Sometimes, egos bunch together as tribes or nations or through rigid religious affiliations to strengthen this sense of 'otherness'.

A group of egos with a cause can be quite a dangerous thing. As we look around us, we see this everywhere: it manifests in politics, nationalism or religion to the point where a bunch of egos who think they are right feel completely justified in killing those they have labelled as wrong. Collectively, all those egos *radiating* fear, anger and other negative states of consciousness infuse the collective consciousness, and it shows up as the chaos and misery endemic on our planet today. Thankfully, many are waking up and *radiating* love, compassion and hope. This, in turn, raises the consciousness of the entire planet.

When things go 'wrong', ego will blame it on the weather, the economy, other people, or germs and bugs. It can believe that it's all down to luck or genes or the ego's 'story'. It can convince us that people don't like us or that we do not deserve good in our lives. The list goes on. No event happens by chance; we are constantly *creating* by our thoughts and *beliefs* and *radiating* out *from* us to *attract to* us the out-picturing of our every thought.

There is a story told of the foreign tourist in Ireland who was asking for directions on how to get to Dublin. An Irishman said to him, "If I were you, I wouldn't start from here!" Using the ego as a starting point to get to unlimited abundance, health and happiness is not the way to go; if the ego believes that it is separate from the abundance or health and happiness, then these qualities cannot be embodied.

Therapy has its uses, but it also has its limitations. The ego working on the ego can only go around in circles. Another ego, that of the therapist, working on one's ego is equally limited. The therapist who reminds you of who you truly are and helps you to connect to the deepest level of your being— your Higher Self—has the best chance of success. This is true healing. The word 'heal' comes from Old English, meaning to *make whole*. So, when we are reminded of who we truly are, we can become *whole* or *healed*. We can return to our original *wholeness.* We are then *complete* and no longer fractured.

Any therapist who tells you that you are 'less than' or 'flawed' can only cause you unnecessary pain and hold back your evolution. Endlessly going over the hurts and traumas of our past is only perpetuating the pain. It is keeping us stuck in the ego's story—the ego's perceived smallness.

If a child is having a nightmare, you don't try to fix the nightmare—you gently wake the child up, and so it is with reality: don't try to fix the illusion, but wake up to the *truth* of who you are. You are a child of Source, a spark of the Divine, Source expressing as you. Waking up from the dream is the only true and real healing. This healing allows the miracles to happen. In the book *The Course in Miracles,* it says, "There is no order of difficulty in miracles". So, no matter how big or how small the problem is, when the truth of who we are dawns on us, the miracles start to happen.

The greatest and highest form of healing any of us can do for each other is to keep reminding one another of the true nature of our being. Waking one another up is the *ultimate* healing and kindness. In fact, it is the *only* kind of healing—all else prolongs the illusion and separation. The very word, *healing*, comes from the root word, *whole.* To *heal* is to make *whole*.

Becoming *whole* is when we reconnect to our Divinity, when we *heal* the fractured Self. It is when we remember who and what we are; that we are Divine, a part of Source, created in the image and likeness of Source. It is to *realise* and to *be* and then to *radiate* our magnificence and our true power. And then, what we *radiate*, we *attract*.

To operate from the Master Self—the *I-AM* Self (hereon in, let us refer to it as 'Higher Self')—is to live the unlimited life. When we say, "For thine is the kingdom, the power, and the glory", we are acknowledging that Source is the true and mighty power that we have access to, because we *are* that power. That power is expressing *as* us when we are expressing from our Higher Power or Higher Consciousness.

This way of thinking is not to kill off the personality self/ego, but rather to allow it to move into its rightful place as witness to the activity of the Divine Higher Self —the *I*. Our aim is to get to the point where the ego admits it does not have all the answers, nor does the ego have the power to change lack to abundance, illness to health, or discord to harmony.

Twelve-step programmes, which have helped millions of hopeless alcoholics and addicts over the last eighty years, include a step that is about handing one's *will* and one's *life* over to the care of a Higher Power. It works. It has saved and changed the lives of millions of people over the last eighty years. That handing over to a Higher Power has caused addicts, drunks and gamblers to recover and to go on to lead happy, fulfilling and meaningful lives.

As we keep our mind focussed on the Higher Self and operate from there and hand our lives over in every respect to this Higher Power, we are then in the state of consciousness where we are experiencing wholeness, abundance, right relations, love, safety, peace and joy. We hand over the reins of government to Higher Self, who knows how to superbly manage, oversee and administer all our affairs. And Higher Self will do it right now.

Consciousness

*"At the centre of your being
you have the answer; you know who you are
and you know what you want".*

—*Lao Tzu*

Consciousness is powerful. Scientists now believe that consciousness existed before matter. As if the ancient masters and teachers have not been telling us that for thousands of years! This is the Age of Consciousness; the Age of Intellect is passing away. The consciousness we are talking about here is knowledge, understanding and awareness—knowledge of who we are, understanding who we are and being aware of who we are. Knowledge, awareness and understanding that we are Source being us.

The more we understand and become aware of that, the more we then become aware that as we *are* Source, we *have* access to all that Source is.

Our sole/Soul purpose on Earth is union with Higher Self and reconnecting with Source, of whom our Higher Self is a part.

To actually manifest the love, abundance, health, harmony and happiness we wish to experience in our lives, we must *be* it. *We must radiate it.* Then, the Law of Attraction will reflect back to us what we are wishing to experience. We are like the projector at the cinema. Life is the screen. What we want to see on the screen has to come from the projector. If we want to see a 'feel-good' romantic movie, then that is what we need to *send* from the projection room. Or, if we like horror films (some do), then we need to put the horror movie in the projector so that it will appear on the screen. We see a clear mental image of that which we wish to have or to experience. We *visualise* what we want, and we then *see* and *feel* the fulfilment of our desire. Then we mentally *radiate* it out into the field of infinite potential—the space all around us.

The field of infinite potential—the universe—picks up and acts on the energy we *radiate* or send out, and that energy *attracts* other similar energies and vibrations that are a vibrational match. We are always at a point of choice. That is where practice and awareness come in. When we first try out this new way of being, we need to be vigilant in our *thoughts*, our *beliefs* and our *beingness*. Like all new habits, it gets easier after a while. Persevere. Do not give up. It will be worth it, I assure you.

We must constantly watch our negative thoughts. They take wings and fly out into the malleable substance of the universe—the field—to join with the great creative power and other situations on that frequency. Then, the universe rearranges the circumstances and *attracts* the people and conditions that we have focussed on to produce the very things we fear. This is where the vigilance comes in. Scientists say that any thought held for more than seventeen seconds takes root and becomes a 'thing'. So, before that seventeen seconds has elapsed, we still have the opportunity to change that thought and replace it with its opposite, then hold on to the new positive thought for seventeen seconds at least and put some feeling into it. *Feelings* magnify the *power* of the *thought*.

Emerson said, "Great hearts send forth steadily the secret forces that incessantly draw great events". Notice he said "steadily". Practice awareness of the great power of Source within, steadily and unwaveringly. And *radiate*—or as he says, *send forth*—that awareness, then life will match or out-picture our vibration.

We must be constant and fearless in our visioning. More prayers than we can possibly imagine were aborted on the very day that they were about to become visible in our lives and our reality. Just because we felt our prayer or *visualisation* was unanswered, we gave up. We also vacillate between believing and doubting. It is like having one foot on the accelerator and one foot on the brake when driving our car: we are going nowhere! A great teacher said, "A kingdom divided against itself shall fall". There can often be a

time lag between our intention and the manifestation of our intention. We need to hold
on to our vision, not with stress or strain, but
with a feeling of positive certainty. And we
need to keep *radiating* our consciousness of
the good we know is ours.

Neither can we force Source to manifest
our desired vision. The sneaky ego may be
the one holding that vision. When we put it
into the care of Source, Source will not give
us something that is not for our greater good.
We must release our vision to Source, not
with a sense of making something happen,
but getting into a state of receiving our good.
More importantly, if we are ill, we need to
adopt a consciousness (or vision) of ourselves
as perfectly well. *Dis*-ease is when we are out
of alignment. Nor should we allow our ego
self to beat ourselves up, as it will tell us we
are failures. We are not failures; we have just
forgotten our perfection for a while.

Our ego may also suggest that if we suffer,
pray hard enough, light candles, chant or
do the right mental gymnastics, then that
'outside god' will give us what we want.
There is no 'outside god' who works for us or

judges whether we deserve our good or not. The best way is to surrender to the Source within and to remember and to know that we already are and have that which we are asking for. It may not yet be visible in the phenomenal world, but it waits for us in the absolute; it waits for us to let go of our fear and accept that which is already ours. So, we bring our mind back to knowing we already are, and therefore have, all that we could possibly desire, and we *radiate* that awareness out into the phenomenal world.

If we are experiencing financial challenges, it is important for us to adopt a consciousness of abundant prosperity, and if experiencing relationship problems and challenges, we need to raise our consciousness to a frequency of love and harmony.

Remember that health, abundance and harmony are the ultimate truth of our being; all else is the illusion created by the ego to keep us in bondage. The nature of Source is perfection and fulfilment. As we are part of Source, that is our nature, too. Anything other is illusion—maya.

Ðow Should We Pray?

"Prayers are the very highest energy
of which the mind is capable".
—Samuel Taylor Coleridge

T here are many techniques and ways of approaching prayer. Much depends on where we are in consciousness.

One way is to align yourself with your Higher Power and release all that relates to your personality—release your name, your gender, your occupation, your status in life, your body, your hopes and dreams, etc. Release all that you feel makes up your human identity. See yourself as an actor in the play of your life, and give up the part you are playing and the costume you are wearing. Take yourself into the space where your heart is. After all, that is the place we point to when we say *me* or *I*. Then become gently and effortlessly aware of the Divine Presence of your Higher Self within.

In the sacred space of our heart, we become aware of the unconditional love and the peace of that omniscient, omnipotent Self that is our true and real Self. There is no need to ask for anything, as our Higher Self knows better than our ego exactly what is best for us and so will never give us anything damaging. We may always *radiate* our vision, but leave the outcome to Source.

> *"If you ask your Father for bread, will he give you a stone; if you ask him for a fish, will he give you a serpent?"*
>
> —*Matthew 11:11*

Keep your mind and your awareness stayed on the Presence, your Higher Self within, and witness the activity of Source working through you. Meditate on this Presence within as the substance and Source that will replenish all that appears to be lacking in your world. *Radiate* love and the joy of knowing that Source is all there is.

Do not strain or struggle. Keep your mind focussed on the inner Divine Presence, and feel the love *radiating* out from you. As you *radiate* out this Divine, omnipotent, omniscient power, the Law of Attraction responds.

Praying successfully is about affecting a change in consciousness. A very effective way to pray is to say "thank you" to the universe/ Source for that which you wish to manifest, even before you have it, and see your wish or desire fulfilled *now*. Because if you see it in the future, it will stay in the future. For example: "Thank you, Source, for my wonderful healing. I am healthy and whole", or: "Thank you, Source, for my financial abundance". Proceed *from* wholeness rather than *towards* it. *Radiate* wholeness. Do not ask. Thank. *Asking* implies lack and need. *Thanking* implies fulfilment and wholeness.

"Therefore I tell you, whatever you ask for in prayer, believe that you have received it, and it will be yours".

—Mark 11:24

Radiate your gratitude. It raises your consciousness to a wavelength of possibility rather than limitation. Remember everything in the universe is energy. All energy is vibrating at different frequencies. We must become a vibrational match to that which we seek so that it can be drawn to us. Lack, disease and disharmony are all vibrating at a low frequency. Gratitude raises us to the frequency of fulfilment, abundance, wholeness and love.

Dr David Hawkins, in his book *Power v Force*, provides a wonderful map of the scale of consciousness. He has done thorough research, and his book is well worth reading with regards to the different levels of consciousness. Our levels of consciousness are the *radiation* we send out that will *attract* the event or state that corresponds to the frequency we are on.

So, it behoves us to do all in our power to raise our consciousness if we wish to experience happiness, health, financial prosperity, loving relationships or any good thing. By doing this, we can truly experience *Heaven on Earth.* Heaven and Hell are not places, but states of mind.

"The course of the world is not predetermined by physical laws. The mind has the power to affect groups of atoms and even tamper with the odds of atomic behaviour".
—Sir Arthur Stanley Eddington
(Mathematician and astrophysicist)

Ðow Ðo We Radiaᴄe?

"Everything in Nature moves in circles.
What goes out must come back. Love and you
will be loved. Extend joy and you will become
more joyful".

—*Ernest Holmes*

We *radiate* by taking on a new form of consciousness: we move from a consciousness of lack to one of abundance. But how do we do that when we have nothing? *Giving* is a sure way to move into the consciousness of *having* abundance. If we have nothing material to give, we can give of our time, our smile, our ear to listen or our love to heal. We can, in meditation, move into that place in our heart where our Spirit dwells and we can see the abundance of Source, of our Higher Divine Self, and we can allow that abundance to *radiate* out from us in all directions. As we *radiate* that feeling of abundance, we cannot fail to *attract* it. It is the Law of the Universe.

Giving demonstrates our *belief* in abundance. Many very rich entrepreneurs follow the practice of *tithing*; that is, of giving one tenth of their income to charity or to their church or an organisation that inspires them. One tenth of one's income may be a bit unrealistic for some, so just give something. *Giving* demonstrates our *belief* in financial abundance. Withholding demonstrates poverty consciousness. If we are feeling a bit stretched financially, going out and buying ourselves a treat gives a clear message to the universe that we *believe* that there will be 'more where that came from'.

Giving thanks is a way of giving. And giving is a way of saying "thank you".

We need to be careful of our mindset and intentions when we are giving. *Giving to get* is not the best consciousness to have when we give. That is ego's way. It still stems from a consciousness of need. Instead, we give as a way of thanking Source for all we have, and we wish to share our love and abundance with others who are part of Source, too. When we give to others, we are really giving to ourselves.

"And the King will answer them, 'Truly I tell you, whatever you did for one of the least of these brothers and sisters of mine, you did for me'".

—Matthew 25:40

In any situation, we need not be afraid to give. We cannot receive anything if we do not give. Take the example of our breath: every time we breathe out, it always comes back. If we hold our breath, we die. We stop the flow. Everything in the universe flows in and out: the seasons, the tides, the movement of the planets. We must keep our abundance moving. We are never diminished by giving.

When we sit and contemplate all that we have and start to be grateful for it, we move into a consciousness of gratitude and plenty. We begin to *radiate* a higher form of consciousness. We move to a new vibration or frequency. On the basis of *like attracts like*, we then find ourselves on the frequency of abundance of all good. We become a vibrational match to that which we desire.

Our gratitude becomes a form of *radiance*. We *radiate* out from us a positive vibration that cannot fail to *attract* its corresponding frequency. *We must radiate to attract,* and we must *radiate* good if we wish to *attract* good. *Radiating* negativity, lack, loss, poverty, anger, lack of love or any other undesirable vibration can only *attract* back to us a matching frequency. It cannot be any other way. It is the Law of Nature.

If we look in the mirror with a scowl and expect to see a smiling face reflecting back at us, it just won't happen. We must have a smile on our face for the reflection to smile back at us. Life is a mirror. It reflects our state of being or state of consciousness right back at us. It cannot be any other way.

Radiate poverty, and life reflects poverty right back at us. *Radiate* riches, and life reflects that back, too. The same is true for all our states of being: love, wealth, health and success. That is what is meant by becoming conscious. For many, that can take a lifetime;

for others, in a 'light-bulb moment', it can all change instantly.

It is all so very simple, but easy it is not. We are creatures of habit, but we are victims of our programming. Most people operate on the default setting of old, negative subconscious beliefs. While they are subconscious, they are extremely difficult to change. Many of these old subconscious beliefs are downloaded to us from our culture, family, religion, education, and the collective consciousness or the friends we keep. We are not even aware of them. Our subconscious makes up 95% of our mind, and we are not aware of it. Not only that, but the subconscious operates at millions more bits per second than the conscious mind does.

Luckily today, we have great therapies that can access and identify our self-harming beliefs, and we can get help to change them. That certainly helps, but rising to Higher Consciousness through meditation and through calling in our Divine Source to help us to erase the old sabotaging beliefs is even more powerful and unfailing. Source is all powerful: *all* powerful.

Pain and suffering can be our best friend and teacher, though we certainly don't think so at the time. Our inner Higher Self will give us these lessons to wake us up. We get to a point where we start to feel 'something has to change—I can't go on like this'. It is then that we seek solutions. Alcoholics or addicts invariably have to hit 'rock bottom' before they will seek help. People who suffer from romance addiction—those always looking for love outside of themselves because they feel unloved and unlovable—will go from one unsatisfactory relationship to another until they hurt so much that they seek help. Then there's the person who just never has enough money no matter how hard they work, until they start to look inside themselves to see that they may, in fact, be the cause of their own problems.

"Your pain is the breaking of the shell that encloses your understanding. Even as the stone of the fruit must break, that its heart may stand in the Sun, so must you know pain. Much of your pain is self-chosen. It is the bitter potion by which the physician within you heals your sick self".
—*Kahlil Gibran*

It is when the pain gets too much that we seek the solution and we start to change. We begin to move from living in the *problem* to living in the *solution*. We learn to focus on the *positive* and take our attention from the *negative*. The pain we encounter is our great teacher. Joseph Campbell referred to it as, "the hero's journey". The hero's journey is the common template of a broad category of tales and lore that involves a hero who goes on an adventure and in a decisive crisis wins a victory, then comes home changed or transformed.

Our crises today may not be that of facing sabre-toothed tigers or defeating dragons. Our 'dragons' today are more commonplace crises and challenges, such as broken relationships, illness, addiction, loss of job, loss of face, etc. As we overcome these challenges, we grow and learn and seek solutions. Like the story of Plato's shadows:

Plato has Socrates describe a group of people who have lived chained to the wall of a cave all of their lives, facing a blank wall. The people watch shadows projected on the wall from objects passing in front of a fire behind them and give names

*to these shadows. The shadows are the prisoners'
reality. Socrates explains how the philosopher is
like a prisoner who is freed from the cave and
comes to understand that the shadows on the
wall are not reality at all, for he can perceive the
true form of reality rather than the manufactured
reality that is the shadows seen by the prisoners.
The inmates of this place do not even desire to
leave their prison, for they know no better life.
The prisoners manage to break their bonds one
day and discover that their reality was not what
they thought it was.*

*They discover the Sun, which Plato uses as an
analogy for the fire that man cannot see behind.
Like the fire that cast light on the walls of the
cave, the human condition is forever bound to the
impressions that are received through the senses.
Even if these interpretations are an absurd mis-
representation of reality, we cannot somehow
break free from the bonds of our human condition—we cannot free ourselves from the phenomenal state, just as the prisoners could not free
themselves from their chains.*

*If, however, we were to miraculously escape our
bondage, we would find a world that we could
not understand—the Sun is incomprehensible*

for someone who has never seen it. In other words, we would encounter another 'realm'—a place incomprehensible because, theoretically, it is the source of a higher reality than the one we have always known; it is the realm of pure form, pure fact.

This is an illustration of the fact that our good is here right now. We just have to wake up and become aware of it. We must step out of the shadows of false illusion and become aware of the reality of the Kingdom of Heaven, which is not in some future place that we may go to when we die but is right here and right now. Heaven is not necessarily a place but a state of consciousness.

Prayer and meditation are the keys, as is a cultivation of the awareness of the Presence within. The Divine Presence of our magnificent Higher Self within can dissolve all error thought patterns. Our Higher Self can, and will, release us from sin. Remember, *sin* is an archery term meaning 'to miss the point'. As we are released from error, we get it, and the more we practice connecting to our inner Higher Self, the better it gets.

It is then that we begin to *radiate* our all good, and the Law of Attraction responds accordingly.

> *"We behold what we are,*
> *and we are what we behold".*
>
> —*Veda Vyasa*
> *The Bhagavad-Gita*

Radiating Financial Abundance

*"If one wishes to demonstrate prosperity, he
must first have a consciousness of prosperity".*
—*Ernest Holmes,*
The Science of Mind

S piritual people very often think that
money is unspiritual. Religion may tell
us that 'money is the root of all evil'. The
pursuit of money may very well be, because
if we are pursuing, we are coming from a
place of lack. Coming from a place of lack
creates competition, as we compete for what
the ego perceives as limited resources. But,
as we *radiate* a consciousness and a knowing
that we already have it because it is ours by

right of the Source-ness we are, we do not have to chase it anymore. We will *radiate* that consciousness and then *attract*.

Money is energy. It is to the life of the planet what the circulatory system is to the life of our body. If the energy in our body becomes congested or blocked, we develop disease. Money, rightly used, can become enlightened energy. If the money supply is blocked in life, it can lead to all kinds of social unrest or even war. Lack of money in society causes hunger and starvation. When people become hungry, they compete for resources; they have no time to enjoy art, beauty, music and other uplifting pleasures. They become impoverished on many levels.

In her book *The Dynamic Laws of Prosperity*, Catherine Ponder says poverty is a sin, caused by mankind's inability to see and accept Source's unlimited givingness. Poverty in our individual lives can cause depression. It contributes to crime, greed, instability, hunger, even disease. There is nothing good about poverty, and the sad part is that we do not have to experience it because all the time we have the Source of wealth right here within us. As previously stated, the original meaning of the word *sin* comes from an archery term and it means to 'miss the point'. The word *repent* means to rethink. So, to *repent* our *sins* is to rethink our erroneous beliefs and bring ourselves back to our innate Source-ness.

Many of us have been brought up with all kinds of ideas about deserving or not deserving financial abundance. Not only do we deserve it, it is ours by right of who we are. It is our birthright and our natural state. Why, then, do we not have it? It is because our ego has cut us off from Source by keeping us separate and limited. The ego does this by telling us that we are not good enough, that we don't deserve, that we have to work hard for it and that it is not good for us. The ego is insane. By connecting with Source and knowing who we truly are, we can bring ourselves back again to remembering our Divine unlimited nature. We are children or offspring of Source, who knows only abundance and actually *is* abundance. So, therefore, we *are* abundance and it is already ours. And we know that Source resides within, not without. *If you don't go within, you will go without!*

Some teachers say we must first *claim* it and then *accept* it. From the position of our Source-ness within, we can even *command* it. To quote the Bible again (I am not a Bible thumper, it is just the teaching I am most familiar with—I'm sure the Koran, the Talmud and the Buddhist teachings all say the same things):

> *"Thou shalt decree a thing, and it shall be established unto thee and the light shall shine upon thy ways".*
>
> —*Job 22:28*

Moses reminded the children of Israel:

> *"Thou shalt remember Jehovah, thy God, for it is he that giveth thee power to get wealth".*
>
> —*Deuteronomy*

The reason there is still so much poverty in our world is that so many do not realise that they must *radiate* to *attract*. They are, in fact, *radiating* the wrong feeling. They are not aware that they have Source within. They do not know that through awareness of and surrendering to the Creator Source within, they have the power to totally change their lives and their circumstances.

Radiating abundance will naturally mean that we do not entertain thoughts of lack or of not having enough. Neither does it mean that we go out and spend all our money extravagantly. Until we reach that state of Consciousness of Wealth on an ongoing basis, we will slip back and forth into Consciousness of Lack. In those 'slips' back into our old, limiting consciousness, we can sabotage ourselves. The Consciousness of Abundance needs to be more than 51% of our awareness before change begins, and as our Consciousness of Abundance becomes the norm, we become abundance. Note *abundance* and not *abundant.* Abundant is a verb describing our state, *abundance* is who we actually *are* because it is obeying the Law of Radiance. New habits and new ways of being need vigilance, and, after a while, this new abundance consciousness becomes who we *are.* Is that why the rich get richer and the poor get poorer?

> *"For unto every one that hath shall be given,*
> *and he shall have abundance: but from him*
> *that hath not shall be taken away even that*
> *which he hath".*
> —*Matthew 25:29*

In other words, if we have (hath) not a Consciousness of Abundance, that which we *have* can even be *taken away* from us. But for those of us who do have a Consciousness of Abundance, *abundance* will be given to us; it is all down to the belief and the state of consciousness that we are *radiating* out from us.

It cannot be easy to *radiate* thoughts of happiness and abundance if one is in a war-torn country and starving. But that is the very time it needs to be *radiated*. Despite the appearances all around, that is when one has to bring in the assistance of a Higher Power to help overcome the ego's experience and to see beyond appearances. It may be that only those who have practiced raising consciousness will be the ones who can reverse this situation. Not many have the faith of Daniel in the lion's den. But Daniel is a great example of one who *created* a miracle to save himself by his faith/*belief*.

Radiating the lower frequencies cannot *attract* the higher frequencies of love, abundance, harmony, health, etc., as the Law of

Correspondences and the Law of Radiance cannot make that vibrational match.

"We are shaped by our thoughts; we become what we think. When the mind is pure, joy follows like a shadow that never leaves".
—*Buddha*

Meditation to Attract Financial Abundance

Find a comfortable place to sit—a place where you will not be disturbed. Take a long, deep breath. Feel that you are breathing in light and harmony.

Take your awareness to the temple of your beautiful sacred heart. Be still. Feel the Presence of your very own Higher Self, the part of you that is part of Source.

Feel the pure, unconditional love that is *you* and *yours*. Ask this Higher Power to help you release all old negative programming regarding your worthiness. Ask to have all limiting beliefs that you are holding anywhere in your energy field now lovingly dissolved.

Then, sit quietly, and become more and more aware of the magnificence and lavish abundance that is the *nature* of your very own *being*. Accept it. Feel it. *Be* it. Sit with it until you begin to know and feel that this is your consciousness of lavish financial abundance.

Then feel yourself *radiating* this awareness out in all directions to imprint on the quantum field of infinite possibility. Feel the gratitude bubble up in your heart for all the blessings that are yours.

This form of prayer is not about pleading with an 'outside god' or trying to force the universe to give us what we want. It is, instead, a releasing of the beliefs in limitation that we have acquired or been taught in our lives. It is a return to *truth*—the *truth* of our *true* Source nature. Master Jesus said, "Know ye not that *ye* are gods and sons of the Most High". It is about correcting our misconceptions.

Radiating and Attracting Love

"Your task is not to seek for love, but merely to seek and find all the barriers within yourself that you have built against it".

—*Rumi*

It is a natural desire of every human being to love and be loved. Babies in orphanages who do not receive human contact and nurturing in the first few months of life do not thrive and often die. Love is to humans as the Sun is to plants. We *are* love. We were created from love. It *sustains* us, and when we are loved, we *flourish*. Like a plant, if we do not get that love, we wither and die.

Negative early conditioning for so many can set up a programme in their consciousness in which they believe that they are unlovable. These are the people who spend their lives looking for love outside of themselves. This seeking for love can often be destructive, with people entering abusive relationships because their level of consciousness is still stuck at the 'unlovable' level. They *radiate* desperation. They also *radiate* the 'I am unlovable' belief that they are carrying. And, as the Law of Radiance sends out this vibration, the Law of Attraction responds by giving them a *reflection* of their *beliefs*. Dysfunctional and damaged people will invariably be *attracted* to other dysfunctional and damaged people. And the pain continues; they get on the merry-go-round of pain and desperation; a merry-go-round that is never very merry.

Some get addicted to love and romance as a way of fixing themselves. Sex addiction is another way that people seek connection and validation, as their concepts of loving and being loved have become warped through childhood or other trauma. This is why there are twelve-step programmes for sex and love addicts anonymous springing up in many cities. Addiction to alcohol, substances, gambling, excessive exercise, shopping, smoking, etc., are all the Soul's desperate seeking for some kind of connection.

One addict described it as 'the hole in the Soul'. Religious folk have sometimes dubbed it 'Divine unrest'. The Soul is desperately seeking the reconnection to Source. Deep within us all, we have a primal memory of our original connection. We are forever seeking it. Original sin is the error that came about when we forgot who we were. Remember, *sin* means to miss the point. But that which we are seeking is not 'out there' somewhere. It is right inside us. It has been there all along.

Our romantic stories and love songs programme us to believe that there is an 'other half' somewhere out there for us to love and be loved by. We develop a deep longing for completion. We feel something is missing. We dream and fantasise that there is a Miss Right or a Mr Right out there who will come into our lives and make it all better, and then we shall live happily ever after.

Could that 'missing piece' be our Divine Self? Deep down, we know that our little ego is not all there is. We know in our heart that something is missing. When we embrace our Divine Self and embody that in our energy field, we get loved from the inside out.

The soulmate illusion thrives in an ego-driven consciousness. We feel we are never enough. Of course we do, because we are incomplete. The ego can never be complete. Only our Higher Self is. We are searching for the Promised Land: the Holy Grail. The thing is, it is already here. It is within us. We become like a dog chasing its tail, when all we need to do is go within. Because that *thing* we are looking for is who we are. That's not to say we can't have a great relationship, but it is best when it is with someone who is awake and is embodying Higher Consciousness.

"Two half people do not make a whole, but two whole people make a beautiful relationship".
—*Anonymous*

In a way to speed up our journey towards that loving and being-loved state of consciousness, there are many belief-change modalities that can help us to release old negative programming from the subconscious and replace them with positive ones. These destructive beliefs are mostly at the subconscious level, and, since our subconscious is more than 95% of our mind, we are often not aware of these negative, destructive programmes that are really running the show. When we identify these hidden, negative programmes and release them, it makes it easier to move into a state of awareness of worthiness and loveableness.

And when we feel loveable, everything changes. We are moving back into that state of love consciousness. And as we *radiate* love, we *attract* love. It is the Law.

One of the primary steps in ascending to Higher Consciousness is to express *unconditional* love. Any love that is conditional is not love at all but something else entirely. That is why love is mentioned so much in the teachings of all the great masters of the many spiritual disciplines through the ages.

When we say such things as, "I will love you if you behave the way I want you to", or, "I will love you if you lose weight", or "I will love you if you stop drinking", or to children, "I will love you if you pass your exams and make me proud", or any other condition we might put on love, then that is not love. That is not to say we should put up with unreasonable behaviour. If a relationship is causing pain and it is not working and we have tried everything, then move on.

Nor should we expect people to change to fit our mould of what we want. That is not love, either. Accept it or leave. We do not have the right to tell others what they should do. We can *ask* them to meet our needs, but we do not have the right to *tell* them. And, remember, just as we are Source expressing as *us*, they are Source expressing as *them*. Source often appears heavily disguised!

Master Jesus said that one of the great problems of humanity was ignorance. Ignorance that he tried to disperse. We are ignorant of our true Self. We assume we are limited. Not only that, but we taught one another the same—in our families, our schools and our institutions. We try to limit the Unlimited and to make the Infinite finite.

The whole issue of loving and being loved is a major issue for humanity. Perhaps it is because we are looking in the wrong place. We are looking outside of ourselves, to other people, to possessions, to pets, to power and status, to excitement, to substances that temporarily give us the illusion that we are okay. These are not lasting solutions. The only lasting solution is the love within us that is the *nature* of our very *being*. We *are* love. All we have to do is realise it, connect to it, and *radiate* it. Then, through the Law of Radiance combined with the Law of Attraction, we *attract* more love than we have ever known. It was always there. It has been waiting for us.

> *"Let a man strive to purify his thoughts.*
> *What a man thinketh, that is he;*
> *this is the eternal mystery.*
> *Dwelling within himself*
> *with thoughts serene, he will*
> *obtain imperishable happiness.*
> *Man becomes that of which he thinks".*
> —*Upanishads*

Meditation to Attract a Loving Relationship

Get into a comfortable position where you know you will not be disturbed. Let all tension melt away. Scan your body to see where you are holding any tension, and let it go.

Ask your Divine Higher Self to help you to release all resentment towards others. And send forgiveness to those you perceive to have hurt you. Feel forgiveness towards yourself for any mistakes you made in the past.

Take yourself into your sacred heart space, and become aware of the Divine Presence within. Become aware of your Source Self. Ask your Divine Self to help you overwrite the ego's fears and doubts.

Oh, dearly beloved Source of my being, I thank You for all the good in my life. I feel Your loving Presence residing right here in my heart. I feel the love. I know that You, who are a part of me, loves me unconditionally. Please help me to love myself unconditionally.

If it is for my greatest good, I now thank You for the wonderful loving Soul who is appearing in my life as a loving companion. I give thanks for the love we feel for one another.

I give thanks for the help and support we are for one another and for all the wonderful times we are enjoying together. We are blessed to be together, and we fit right into one another's lives. We laugh together, we grow together and we are there for one another in every way.

Thank You. Thank You. Thank You.

It is now in your Higher Power's hands, so do not keep going over and over it endlessly and wondering when and how and who. That is none of your business!

Say this prayer daily with faith and love. Remember to always get yourself in a state of love, expectancy and certainty as you say the prayer. Try not to waver.

Wavering is keeping your foot on the brake, and certainty keeps your foot on the accelerator. Both at the same time means nothing can happen. Get out of the driving seat, and let Source take over.

Radiating Perfect Health and Wholeness

*"Matter is Spirit moving slowly enough
to be seen".*
—*Pierre Teilhard di Chardin*

In quantum physics, everything is either a wave or a particle. A wave can become a particle, and a particle can become a wave. Our bodies are waves of pure energy or Spirit that has become solid particles. Our bodies are a material expression of our Soul or Spirit. They are surrounded and interpenetrated by the etheric, emotional, mental and cosmic energies of a force field. It reflects our state of consciousness. Our bodies can be a symbol of separation because those who identify only with the physical cannot have any understanding of themselves as beings of light or expressions of Divine energy.

Our cells are made up of atoms. Atoms are made up of electrons, protons and neutrons. Those atoms are like mini solar systems with the electrons, protons and neutrons swirling about. In fact, atoms are 99.9999% empty space. So, therefore, they are only 0.0001% matter. All that space! What is in that 'empty' space? Information. Consciousness. That 'empty' space is the important bit. It can be influenced directly by our *thoughts* and our *beliefs*.

Major breakthroughs in quantum physics, genetics and cutting-edge psychology are all available to us now to free us from being victims of circumstance. We were always told that our genes were responsible for our make-up and consequently our health and longevity, and because there was no other evidence available until now, we believed that idea. And many still subscribe to it. There is now a whole new theory emerging called 'epigenetic theory'. This theory proposes that our genes and their expression can be directly affected by environmental factors. Genes, they propose, can be turned on and off.

Epigenetic theory views human development as the result of an ongoing bidirectional interchange between heredity and environment. Environmental influences include family dynamics, schooling, relationships, accidents we have had, traumas and diseases we have suffered, and much more.

Genes do not turn themselves on and off; the environment does that. The status or combination of turned-on and turned-off genes is known as the 'epigenome'—that is, the overall condition or state of the cell.

In his revolutionary book on epigenetics *The Biology of Belief,* renowned cell biologist Bruce H. Lipton describes and demonstrates how the new understanding of the link between mind and matter is profoundly affecting our understanding of how our genes work. He shows how our genes and DNA do not control our biology but instead how DNA is controlled by signals from outside the cell, including the energetic messages emanating from our positive or negative thoughts: our consciousness. To believe that our genes are the cause of our disease is to be a victim, to believe that we have no control over our own bodies or our destiny. To understand and to know that the scientific evidence is there to prove otherwise is empowering.

It also puts the ball back firmly in our own court—we are responsible for our own biology by our *thoughts*, *feelings* and *beliefs*. In other words, by our consciousness.

What a liberating bit of information that can be. The buck stops here! With you and me. Change our thoughts, change our beliefs, and we change our consciousness. To achieve perfect, dynamic, radiant health, we must develop a consciousness of it. We must switch from focusing on illness and what is wrong to health and what is right.

Ageing is another limiting and totally unnecessary belief that limits us. Our bodies are made up of zillions of cells. Those cells are constantly renewing themselves. If our cells are constantly dying off and constantly renewing themselves, why would they renew themselves with old worn-out cells?

Our bodies have intelligence. So why would our bodies do something as stupid as replace dying cells with cells that were less than perfect? It is because we tell them to. We do not consciously tell them to, but in our thinking patterns and our individual and collective beliefs, we are sending our cells that message all the time, and so many of these messages are the negative ones we have downloaded into our minds from a very early age.

We are so used to sending out that message that it has become automatic and we do not consciously think about it anymore. We are like those who once believed that the Earth was flat. It was perfectly obvious to them—all they had to do was look around them. Their eyes and vision told them that they were standing on flat ground. They had no way of knowing that the Earth was round. They would, and did, think that anyone who thought that the Earth was anything other than flat was barking mad.

We have fallen into the pattern of thinking that because we are getting older in years, we must also suffer from the deterioration of ageing and that anyone who suggests otherwise... must be barking mad!

As we nurture and develop a *consciousness* of perfect health, vitality and wholeness, we *radiate* that awareness throughout our entire physical body, and it responds. Through the Law of Radiance, as we *radiate* a *consciousness* of health and wellbeing, the Law of Attraction must respond. It is the Law. The Source and consequent manifestation of our physical body is an intelligent one. We are designed to express perfect health and vitality. It is our birthright and our natural state of being.

Medication to Radiate Perfect Health and Wholeness

"Every human being is the author of his own health or disease".

—*Buddha*

Sit in a comfortable place where you will not be disturbed. Close your eyes.

Take your awareness into your heart, and see the shining light of your Higher Self there. Touch your heart centre if it helps to bring your attention there.

Feel the love in your heart. Or feel the gratitude in your heart. Whatever you feel there, make sure it is a feeling on a high frequency—love, gratitude, joy, compassion.

The heart centre is the dwelling place of our Higher Self or Higher Consciousness. In the chakra system, the heart is the centre of the seven chakras where the force field crosses to form a powerhouse of etheric energy.

The HeartMath Institute has done an immense amount of research into the amazing power of the heart, and Gregg Braden has written extensively about it.

"Your heart's intelligence is with you always. It is constant. You can trust it. It is important to acknowledge this, because it means that the wisdom of your heart—the answers to the deepest and most mysterious questions of life that no one else can answer—already exist within you".

Know that Source/your Higher Self is the Creator and Source of your physical body. Source/Higher Self is perfect. Let that idea of perfection *radiate* out into every cell of your physical body. See it moving through your entire being. Visualise it as light if that helps. It *is* light. We are beings of light.

Let that light of Source perfection flow to any part of your body that you feel is less than whole and perfect, and see the error belief being gently and lovingly eradicated. *Radiate* that perfection, and as the Law of Radiance sends out its rays of perfect youthfulness, health and wellbeing, the Law of Attraction will *reflect* back that perfection to your physical being.

Feel the light and the love of your Higher Self—your *true* and only *real* self—flowing through you. Feel yourself filling with gratitude as you *radiate* this perfection from the centre of your *true*, loving Higher Self. Feel that gratitude while your good is still invisible. Your good is present in the unmanifested state, and, as it is energy vibrating at a very fast pace, it has to be slowed down to appear in the lower frequency of the *visible* physical world. There may be a time lapse.

Give thanks for a perfect, healthy, vital body, even if it is not representing its true nature at the moment. The more you practice *radiating* this consciousness of health and wellbeing, the more the cells of your body will respond and will out-picture the vibration of wellbeing, youthfulness and vitality. Remember, our cells are renewing themselves all the time, and as you take on the frequency of health, the new cells will exhibit that state of being. Our physical body will always reflect our innermost beliefs and state of consciousness. *Radiate* a consciousness of health and wellbeing, and as the Law of Radiance beams out this perfect state, the Law of Attraction will *reflect* back that state of perfection. It has to. It is the Law.

"The moment you change your perception, is the moment you rewrite the chemistry of your body".
—Dr Bruce Lipton PhD
(Cellular biologist and research scientist)

'Science of Mind' Prayer

'Science of Mind' is the non-religious spiritual teaching of Dr Ernest Holmes. It has no connection with Scientology.

My body was designed by an infinite Intelligence to heal quickly and naturally.

No condition regardless of appearance can stop or slow the natural healing process that is taking place now.

Since healing knows nothing of time, it does not require time.

Prayer repair is underway and cannot be stopped by fear, doubt, outside conditions or appearances.

Purpose and Right Livelihood

"Riches are not from an abundance of worldly goods but from a contented mind".

—*Muhammad*

To be happy and fulfilled in all aspects of our lives is important. Finding our niche in the area of our career is essential if we are to have a full, rounded-out life of contentment and satisfaction. We spend a major part of our waking day in our workplace. Multiply that by hours in the week and weeks in the year, and we see what a major part of our lives is spent in the workplace. How important it is, then, to look at the concept of whether we are happy and fulfilled spending time doing what we do.

Research has shown that the majority of people are not happy in their job. How sad is that? Source's children are surely not meant to live like that. When we begin to wake up and remember who we truly are, we also begin to question the fundamentals such as "am I happy in my work?" We realise that we need to change. That is when the ego pipes up with all sorts of objections, like telling us we are "too old to change", we have "not got enough qualifications", we will "lose our pension", it is "not easy these days to get a new job", "the market is slow", "there is a recession", or a multitude of other excuses for not taking a leap of faith and trusting our Higher Self, the Source part of us, to take charge and to provide all we need. The ego does not like change because it fears it may lose its grip. By keeping us in a consciousness of limitation, our ego stays in charge.

Of course, it is scary to take a risk, and it should not be taken lightly, but is it not scarier to contemplate a life of slavery in the daily grind of doing a job we hate or, at best, endure? Honouring our desire for a more fulfilling occupation is where we can make a great stride forward in our development and in our trust and belief in who and what we really are. Taking our time at this is vital because if we have not arrived at that place of consciousness yet where we completely know and truly embody our consciousness of the power within us, we are not quite ready to take that big step just yet. We could, in fact, set ourselves back quite a bit.

So, it is important to keep on making that daily conscious connection with Source, putting out our vision of what we would really like to do and then *radiating* that Higher Consciousness out into, and onto, the field of infinite possibility that is the quantum field around us. If we do not quite know what it is we actually want to do, we have only to ask Higher Self/Source to show us the way. Source always wants the best for its children. When we were children, we very often knew instinctively what we wanted to do because we exhibited certain talents at an early age. Society then stepped in and educated us out of following our heart's desire.

One of the best ways we can communicate with our Source is to ask, "How can I be of service?" Being of service then gets us in line with our purpose. Our 'being of service' does not have to be something grandiosely spiritual; it could be starting our own business making pies, or going back into education to be a lawyer or a nurse or a doctor. Or it might be becoming a train driver, if that is what we always wanted.

When we move into this consciousness of fulfilment and wholeness in our lives, and when we align ourselves with our almighty Higher Self, we will be guided to do the right thing, to go to a certain place or to perform a certain task.

Being aware of the promptings of our Higher Self is how we strengthen our connection. The guidance will invariably come from our feeling *nature*; we will feel it in our heart. Sometimes, it may come in a dream or in our meditations, or we may hear it from someone else or find it in a book. The key is to be *aware*. Source is communicating with us all the time. Let us not close the channels.

When we have consciously surrendered the management of all our affairs to Source, Source will open the doors of opportunity for us. Source will guide us to the right job, to the right course of education or to the right course of action. The Higher Self sees the big picture. Of course, when we hand our lives over to this awesome power, we cannot sit on our backsides—we must move into guided action. We develop an awareness. We listen to the inner promptings. Then we *ACT*.

> *"My profession is the activity of*
> *the Great Mind working through me".*
> —*Ernest Holmes*
> *The Science of Mind*

The little *i* (the ego) gets caught up on the *how*. We ask ourselves *how* is this good going to happen? Leave the *how* to the Higher Self. Think of it as sat nav/GPS. We want to go to a place in our car where we have never been before. We have no idea how to get there. But we do not have to worry; we just programme the desired destination into the sat nav/GPS. This is our Divine Higher Self. It has all the info and sees the big picture.

So, we set up the destination, put it into the sat nav/GPS, and then we let go. Like driving our car, we trust the navigation system, but we have to do the footwork, like getting behind the wheel, obeying the traffic laws, driving consciously and listening to the navigation system's vocal commands. That is the still, small voice of our inner Higher Self when we are on the road to abundance, health and joy.

Abundance embraces wealth, health, right livelihood, harmonious relationships, fun and enjoyment. When we are conscious and in alignment with Source, we can truly experience Heaven on Earth. To do so, we must make every effort to improve our *conscious* contact with Source. We can never be without unconscious contact or we would not exist, but it is the *conscious* contact that really makes the difference.

Meditation to Find Purpose and Right Livelihood

As with all meditations, find a quite place where you are unlikely to be disturbed. Get yourself in a comfortable position, scan your body for where you feel any tension or tightness, and just let it go.

Be aware of the rhythm of your breathing; let it become slow and relaxed. If thoughts are running around in your head, observe them but do not hang on to them. Keep bringing your attention back to your breathing.

Breathe evenly and slowly. Bring your attention to your heart space. See the inner light of your Divine Source within. Be aware of that light, and feel the love—the unconditional love.

As far as you are able, let all cares and worries fall away. Begin a dialogue with your Higher Divine Self, the part of you that is a fragment of Source and containing all of Source.

You may find your own words, but here are some suggested ones:

Beloved Source of my being, I give thanks for all that I have and for the opportunities I have been given. I give thanks for my life, my mind, my understanding, and for the love You have shown me.

I know that You know my requests even before I ask. I now ask Your help in changing my career path. I ask for Your inspiration on how, when and where to make my next move. I wish to be of service in whatever way You think will benefit me and benefit all with whom I come into contact.

I await Your Divine guidance and inspiration. I thank You in advance for the wonderful new opportunities coming my way.

Thy will, not mine, be done.

This form of prayer is not about pleading with an 'outside god' or trying to force the universe to give us what we want. It is, instead, a releasing of the beliefs in limitation that we have acquired or been taught in our lives. It is a return to *truth*. The *truth* of our *true* Source nature. Master Jesus said, "Know ye not that *ye* are gods and sons of the Most High". It is about correcting our misconceptions.

Common Questions

"Reality is merely an illusion, albeit a very persistent one".

—*Albert Einstein*

Science

In our modern world, we love science. It has become our 'god'. If science says something is true, then we believe that it must be true. If science says it is not true, then we adopt that as our perception.

For a long time, western science has been worshipping at the altar of classical physics. The old Newtonian scientific paradigm known as 'classical physics' saw our bodies as mindless machines. Our medical systems, until very recently, used this premise to treat disease. In the past eighty years, quantum physics has come to the fore and a whole new understanding of reality has emerged. The weight of scientific evidence is toppling the old paradigm.

As already mentioned, at the quantum level in physics, everything is either a wave or a particle. The wave only becomes a particle when it is witnessed. This is where our Source-given creative power comes from. Nothing *has* any reality until we *give* it reality. On an everyday level, it all comes back around to 'what we focus on, we get more of'. Focus on the negative, we get a negative outcome. Focus on the positive, and we get positive outcomes. Whatever level of consciousness we *radiate* at, we will *attract* its vibrational match. Constant vigilance and awareness are, therefore, vital to our maintaining and *radiating* the level of *consciousness* of the state of being or the thing we wish to *attract*. It is important to never give attention to that which we *do not* want.

As the new physics emerges, it becomes evident that it is not dissimilar to the teachings of the mystics and sages, especially of eastern culture and philosophy.

Everlasting Life

The masters promised us everlasting life, and this teaching has lost them some credibility among those who do not understand—those who see life only from the ego's point of view.

When the masters spoke of 'eternal life', they did not, of course, mean the life of the ego and the limited physical plane. If our consciousness is purely on the physical plane of the ego's perception, then there is no everlasting life. The masters taught us that when we raise our consciousness beyond ego limitation, we connect to the Divine Higher Self. We return to Higher Self/Source consciousness where there is no death. Source is eternal. Death as we know it belongs only to the physical plane.

As the poet Longfellow put it so eloquently: "Dust thou art, to dust returneth, was not spoken of the *Soul*". We are more than the solid matter we think we are. We are pure Spirit—light frequencies stepped down to appear solid. We have become seduced and enamoured of the physical; trapped in an illusory reality. Maya. Making the shift in consciousness takes us to a whole new level, where we see through the ego's deception and we become the Witness Self. Witnessing the drama but not engaging in it. Seeing it for what it is.

While on the physical plane, our bodies are the house of our Higher Self. Christianity refers to the body as 'the temple of the Holy Spirit'. The body, therefore, must be cherished and cared for. There have been various sects throughout the ages who so abhorred the body and its ego connection that they lacerated it by flogging themselves with whips that had nails on the end of the thongs, or they starved themselves or wore hair shirts to punish the body. They missed the point entirely that it is not the body but the state of consciousness that causes the problems, and that is what needs to be changed. They missed the point that the body is *sacred*, not in and of itself, but as the *home* and the temple of the Divine aspect of our being.

Let us love our body in this context, that the body itself is not who we are. We live in it. We *radiate* through it and we *radiate* from the sacred space of our heart. We are tourists here on planet Earth. We have an innate longing to return home. We intuitively know that there is more. Our journey here is that of Source expressing All-That-Is. To long to 'go home' is not to long for physical death but to long for reconnection to Higher Self/Source. We can do that while we are here. Not only can we do it, but as we do it, we can achieve that 'Heaven on Earth' that was promised by the masters.

As we *radiate* our Divine nature, we infuse matter with Spirit. As we raise our own consciousness, we contribute to the raising of consciousness for all of creation because we are *connected* to *everyone* and *everything*. We accelerate the journey home. Home is where the heart is, as they say. It is not a place. Home is a return to a remembrance or a consciousness of the *truth* of our *being*. Home is where the Father/Source resides and to where the prodigal son returns to share in the bliss of Heaven while still here on Earth, and to enjoy everlasting life.

Karma

So, where does karma fit into all of this? Is there not a 'Law of Karma'? And if there is, how can we rise above the results of our misdemeanours?

Karma means action, work or deed; it also refers to the spiritual principle of cause and effect where intent and actions of an individual influence the future of that individual.

In other words, what we put out, we get back. This is really the Law of Radiance in action. What we *radiate* out into the world, we get back. As we raise our consciousness to a place of harmlessness, we come to a place of peace and harmony. We hand our will and our lives over to a Higher Power—our Divine Source Self. And on this level, there is no karma. Karma is cancelled out. Karma is for the ego or personality self.

However, every time we slip back into ego self, we are self-centred and descend to the frequencies of the lower aspects of our consciousness, where we express anger, jealousy and competition. In fact, we are likely to exhibit all of the seven deadly sins. We move back down to ego level and lose

touch with the true source of our power—
our Source/Higher Self. Then karma comes
into force.

Once we come to full (not partial) recog-
nition of our oneness with Source, further
learning on the physical plane becomes
superfluous. We then do not need to con-
tinue on the wheel of birth and rebirth.

On the level of Higher Self/Source is
where we find all of the good that we are
heir to and which has always been ours
by our Divine birthright. Relationships
with others can be the most potent trig-
ger points that drag us right back down to
ego level to experience limitation all over
again. When we begin to express jealousy,
blame, criticism, anger, judgement, etc., we
lower our frequency and we lose that beautiful connection with Source. When we are
radiating negative feelings towards others
and are harming another living creature, we
become disconnected from the frequency of
Source. We drop down to a lower frequency
and *radiate* that frequency to *attract* a vibrational match of people, situations and things

that are on a correspondingly low frequency. *Like attracts like.*

Like many other habits, operating from ego is a habit. Like all habits, it can be changed, but it takes vigilance and discipline. As the ego does not want to lose its grip, it will tell us, "Oh, forget it, it is all too hard". Or when things begin to improve because we have been practising the Presence of Higher Self/Source, the ego may say, "Things are okay now. I'll handle the rest from hereon in". The ego is devious and will do all it can to stay in power. It is not easy to change entrenched habits and behaviours, but it can be done. Like many other disciplines, it gets easier the more we do it, and the rewards are great!

"The awakening is finally realising that you are a part of God, like a single cell that finally sees it is a part of you".

—L J Vanier

Waking Up

*"A global awakening can only happen
from a spiritual awakening that is of
global dimensions".*

—*Matthew Fox*

S ource is here on this plane, expressing
in a variety of ways, sometimes so downloaded to ego level that it is hard to see the
Source within. But it is there. Sometimes it is
so well hidden that we have a problem seeing
it. Neither should we judge. The one we perceive has lost his or her way and has become
so ego driven that they do not have any consciousness of their Higher Source/Self. Such
a person deserves our love and light far more
than the saint. The saint has no need of our
love—they are love. The lost Soul who is

not awake is the one who deserves our love and needs our love. As we mentally send our unconditional love to them, it will help to wake them up.

"Out beyond ideas of wrongdoing and rightdoing,
there is a field, I'll meet you there.
When the soul lies down in that grass,
the world is too full to talk about.
Ideas, language, even the phrase "each other"
doesn't make any sense".

—*Rumi*

So, it is up to us—each one of us individually—to take responsibility for our own growth, and, as we do, we add to the collective consciousness of the whole. On some level, there is only one of us; we are all cells in one great body of creation, and the best thing we can do for others is raise our own consciousness.

We can only save ourselves—each one of us. It is through saving ourselves that we save the whole. We are all cells in one great *being*. To put the saving of others first is taking responsibility for others' growth and evolution and is, therefore, co-dependency. By all and every means, we help everyone we can but without imposing or interfering. A great teacher once said, "I am not my brother's keeper". In the *light* of today's *knowledge*, we now have an understanding of that statement.

"Let there be peace, but let it begin with me".
—*Gandhi*

We must start right *here*, in our own consciousness, and *heal* our separation from Source by remembering who we are. We must move to expressing our own Divine Self and diminish the power of the ego. Like Mother Teresa, we must see the Divine in all others, too, and, if given the opportunity, gently and kindly remind them of who they really are.

As each of us heals ourselves and operates from Higher Self rather than from ego, then and only then can we heal the world. Embrace the ego, too. It is part of us. Let us embrace the ego, but make sure that the Higher Self is in charge. Step into our power. Remember our Source-ness.

As we actually become—or should we say 'return to'—our Higher Selves, then love, health and abundance of all kinds *must* be the *nature* of our *reality*. As the power of the ego, and all the other egos, falls away, so do fear and greed and war and want. The latter are all constructs of the ego.

The Higher Self—and remember all our Higher Selves are part of the One Self/Source and the One Higher Self—knows only perfection. As this One Higher Power is unlimited, we can, as one, perform miracles.

Now is the time of the great awakening. When we look around and see the appearance of chaos, we may be filled with dismay. But think again. Could it not be the last desperate stand of the ego, and all the egos who see the writing on the wall, as we start to remember who we really are? All the doubts and fears of the ages are coming to the surface to be cleared away once and for all time.

This is a time of remembering our *glorious origin*; a time of healing the separation. We stand on the threshold of a golden era.

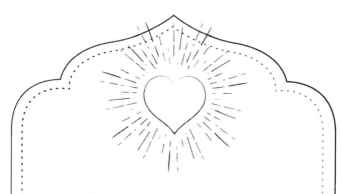

A Sleep of Prisoners

The human heart can go the lengths of God.
Dark and cold we may be, but this
Is no winter now. The frozen misery
Of centuries breaks, cracks, begins to move;
The thunder is the thunder of the floes,
The thaw, the flood, the upstart Spring.

Thank God our time is now when wrong
Comes up to meet us everywhere,
Never to leave us till we take
The longest stride of soul man ever took.

Affairs are now soul size.
The enterprise
Is exploration into God.
Where are you making for? It takes
So many thousand years to wake,
But will you wake, for pity's sake?

— Christopher Fry

About the Author

Anne M. Hassett has been involved in the field of spirituality, personal growth and self-awareness for thirty-nine years. An experienced spiritual counsellor and intuitive coach, Anne has a huge following worldwide and counts clients from both the worlds of showbiz and the aristocracy among her many clients.

Better known by many as Acushla, she studied for a degree in metaphysics under Dr Douglas Baker. Acushla also has a deep and lasting relationship with twelve-step programmes.

Dedicated to her life mission, which is to empower people, help them to take responsibility for their lives and to support them in becoming masters of their own destiny rather than victims, Acushla runs courses, workshops and retreats all over the world. She is a published author of several books.

She is also a Reiki master, metaphysician, spiritual teacher, fingerprint and hand analyst, rebirther, author and broadcaster.

Read more at www.AcushlasAngels.com.

Other Books
by the Author

READING YOUR CHILD'S HAND
Discover Your Child's Talents and Abilities

DISCOVER THE INNATE
POTENTIAL OF CHILDREN
... And They Will Love You
Co-written with Marianne Volonté

DYNAMIC AGELESS YOU
Belief shapes Biology
So... GIVE YOURSELF A FAITH-LIFT!

THE POWER OF SAYING F*** IT!
Letting Go and Letting God

ANGEL WHISPERS

Available on Amazon and
www.shop.AcushlasAngels.com

Suggested Readings

EMPOWERMENT
by John Randolph Price

ILLUSIONS
by Richard Bach

THE FIELD
by Lynne McTaggart

THE NATURE OF PERSONAL REALITY
by Jane Roberts

YOU ARE THE KEY
by Shaun de Warren

FIND AND USE YOUR INNER POWER
by Emmet Fox

THE ISAIAH EFFECT
by Gregg Braden

GOD I AM
by Peter O Erbe

Printed in Great
Britain
by Amazon

32142161R00085